So, You Want to Be Canadian

11/5/2014

All About
THE MOST FASCINATING PEOPLE
IN THE WORLD
and THE MAGICAL PLACE
THEY CALL HOME

KERRY COLBURN & ROB SORENSEN

ILLUSTRATIONS BY S.BRITT

CHRONICLE BOOKS
SAN FRANCISCO

Library of Congress Cataloging-in-Publication Data available.

ISBN-10: 0-8118-4535-4
ISBN-13: 978-0-8118-4535-9

Manufactured in **CANADA**
Printed on recycled paper

Designed by Sara Gillingham, a Canadian!

10 9 8 7

Chronicle Books LLC
680 Second Street
San Francisco, California 94107
www.chroniclebooks.com

For Canadians everywhere
Pour tous les Canadiens

You're the best, eh?

Greetings from CANADA!

LEARN HOW TO

TAP YOUR TOES

MEET

Hockey!

Mounties

and so much more....

a primer

Canada
The Land of Dreams

EVERYBODY wants to be Canadian! And why not, eh?
Imagine a vast and magical country where the locals
are good-looking, the beer is tasty, and the living is easy.
If you always thought that "neighbor to the north" meant
Alaska, or the people living in the apartment upstairs,
you've got a lot to learn about Canada (isn't learning fun?).

Did you know that . . .

 Canadians are the most fascinating people alive.

 Hockey provides nearly year-round excitement
and joy.

 You can go to the hospital if you're sick.

 Anyone can marry anyone.

 The scenery is beautiful, the water is clean,
and the food is delicious.

 Pot is pretty much legal.

It's no surprise that beer and beavers and Mounties and moose make for an intoxicating smorgasbord of delights. But there's so much more. Did you know that Canadians invented both the zipper *and* ginger ale? That Neil Young, Joni Mitchell, and Leonard Cohen are all 100 percent Canadian? That Canadians were the first to play ice hockey? That the beautiful American west you see in many movies is actually Canada? That the handles on Canadian beer cases are big enough to fit your hands with mittens on? Those Canadians aren't just polite, they're darn clever.

Inside this helpful book, you'll find a multitude of fascinating facts about what makes Canada the most glorious of nations. From how to make *poutine* to how to say "toque," from how to use hockey terms in the bedroom to the difference between a loonie and a toonie, you'll get all the ins and outs of being a Canadian—even if you aren't. So whether you're a true-blue Canuck, or just wish you were, you can read on to discover what makes the Great White North so great. Beauty, eh?

Canada:
Where Is It?

Canada is located directly to the north of the United States on the continent of North America and is host to nearly thirty-two million residents known as "Canadians." Within its whopping ten million square kilometers of space is a wonderland of scenic wilderness, cosmopolitan cities, and non-stop excitement. Come along as we explore this peaceful and benevolent kingdom that the natives call "Canada."

Welcome

Northwest Territories

Yukon Territories

Nunavut

British Columbia

Saskatchewan

Manitoba

Alberta

12

to *Canada*

New Brunswick

Newfoundland

MAPLE SYRUP

Nova Scotia

Prince Edward Island

Quebec

Ottawa
The Nation's
Capital

Ontario

13

10 Provinces to Know and Love—
and Three Territories to Cuddle With

Provincial Flower
Pacific Dogwood

British Columbia: Never a dull moment in fun-filled B.C., where hippies and hipsters sail, smoke, ski, and happily drink to Canada's coolest (not coldest) province.

Provincial Flower
Wild Rose

Alberta: It's no wonder Texas is called "the Alberta of the U.S." Big steers and black gold make this beefy province the last bastion of real cowboys and range-riding before the slide into liberal, hemp-happy B.C.

Provincial Flower
Prairie Lily

Saskatchewan: The province where you can watch your dog run away for three days—expansive, sleek Saskatchewan doesn't bother with mountains, but concentrates on raising hockey players, and people who can spell "Saskatchewan."

Provincial Flower
Prairie Crocus

Manitoba: Here in Canada's heartland, Manitobans celebrate having the coldest intersection in the country—Portage & Main in Winnipeg, immortalized by many Canuck musicians, including 'Pegger Neil Young in the song "Prairie Town"—and for having a town called Flin Flon. (It's fun to say!)

Ontario: Canada's political elite, corporate bigwigs, and blue-collar industrialists rub elbows in this cosmopolitan province. It's home to the nation's capital, Ottawa, and its biggest city, Toronto—known affectionately as "New York without the garbage" and "London with better teeth."

Quebec: Lovingly deemed "Canada's smoking section," Quebec overflows with European culture, architecture, accents, and of course, *poutine* (see page 67). Rumors of its secession have been greatly exaggerated—although feisty and independent-minded, Quebec is still firmly part of Canada. Hydroelectric power is Quebec's gift to the Northeast and Celine Dion its gift to the world. (Oh yes, and maple syrup.)

Did You Know?

Quebec's Ice Hotel, unique in North America, is built anew each winter from ice and snow and disappears by spring.

New Brunswick:

The only officially bilingual province in Canada, this quiet, unassuming little brother stays out of the limelight except once every twelve hours, when it shows off with the mind-blowing tides of Fundy. (Well, that happens in Nova Scotia, too, but whatever.)

Nova Scotia:

Seafood and sailing reign supreme in Nova Scotia. So climb aboard and fill your gullet with Digby scallops and lobsters bigger and cheaper than in Maine. If you don't understand a word someone is saying, you've met an Acadian, the Canadian equivalent to the Cajun. (Well, that happens in New Brunswick, too, but whatever.)

Prince Edward Island:

A teeny, tiny island covered in rich, red muck, Prince Edward Island is proud of its two famous exports, *Anne of Green Gables* and potatoes, the latter celebrated in song by Canadian folk hero Stompin' Tom Connors: "Bud the spud from the bright red mud rolling down the highway smilin', the spuds are big on the back of Bud's rig and they're from Prince Edward Island" (see page 49).

Newfoundland/Labrador: Like the friendly dogs of the same name, folks from this province are loveable, frisky, often wet, and loyal at all costs. "Newfs," as they're affectionately called, are appreciated all the more for graciously stepping forward in their waders to become the constant punchline of the country's jokes (so that no one had to make fun of foreigners).

Yukon Territories: Generously allowing Alaska its breathing room, this Gold Rush territory rests just above B.C., providing solace to America's fiftieth state when, like a lost puppy, it longs to snuggle up to something familiar.

Northwest Territories: Despite the record cold, residents here are amazingly nimble-tongued, speaking no less than eight official languages—Chipewyan, Cree, Dogrib, English, Gwich´in, Inuktitut, Slavey, and French. (Yes, French!)

Nunavut: Already sparking the cheer "I'll have Nunavut!" this frosty new baby of Canada became a territory in 1999, and is the best place in the country to trip-out on Northern Lights. (That, and a really good snow cone.)

Royalty and Democracy:

CANADA GOES BOTH WAYS

Although originally a British colony, Canada—unlike its bratty little brother—gently and politely declared its independence from Mother England over time. Today, Canada enjoys the best of both worlds: A constitutional monarchy that offers the pomp and tradition of royalty plus all the modern benefits of a democracy. ("Off with their heads!" "Er, can we vote on that?") As Canadians know, it's glamorous and exciting being part of royalty, complete with an honest-to-goodness Queen, who benevolently rules from afar (and who also bravely dropped the puck at a Vancouver Canucks game, as part of her 2002 Golden Jubilee).

Did You Know?

A. A. Milne named Winnie the Pooh after a bear seen at the London Zoo—but the bear was not a Brit, it was a Canadian cub brought over by a veterinarian joining the Canadian Infantry Brigade during the First World War, who named it for his hometown of Winnipeg.

Some perks of being part of the British Commonwealth:

 No arguments about who appears on the currency (it's the Queen, silly)

 Easy off-shore scapegoat

Opportunities to bow and curtsy

A nice foil for dental comparison (Canucks have better "teef")

Commonwealth Games—a chance to compete and party with fellow drinkers, including Australia, Jamaica, India, and New Zealand

The Plot to Keep Canada Small

Nice try, but you can't keep Canada down! Often wrongly depicted as dark and diminutive on U.S.—issued classroom maps, Canada is actually very big . . . and bigger is better.

figure 1.

figure 2.

THE CANADIAN INDEX

Number of Americans for every Canadian: **9**

Number of square kilometers of extra elbow room per person Canada enjoys, compared to the United States: **62,010**

Amount that Canada is larger in territory to the United States, expressed in terms of number of hockey rinks: **33,345,403**

Number of laps needed to jog the coastline of the United States to equal a lap around Canada's coastline: **10**

Number of Canadian television viewers who tuned in for the 1972 "Summit on Ice" hockey final between the Soviets and the Canadians, more than did for Neil Armstrong's moon walk: **2,500,000**

Average number of extra days lived by a Canadian, as opposed to an American: **836**

Number of times the United States invaded Canada: **2**

Number of times Canada successfully defended itself: **2**

Canadian Timeline

Great Moments of a Great Country

40,000 B.C.   First settlers arrive from Asia via Beringia, the land bridge connecting Siberia to Alaska.

Circa A.D. 985   Norsemen see and settle in what is known today as Newfoundland. Rumors that screech, a powerful Newf liquor (see page 74), caused the demise of the settlement are unsubstantiated.

Jun. 24, 1497   John Cabot lands on the Canadian coast and claims it for England.

May 2, 1670   Much to the chagrin of the North American beaver, fur-trader and entrepreneur Prince Rupert is granted permission to create the Hudson's Bay Company, the first company in North America.

Sept. 13, 1759 The Battle of the Plains of Abraham results in French Canada succumbing to the English colonies. Both generals die, but *poutine* and that saucy French attitude survive.

Dec. 31, 1775 The American invasion of Canada fails because the French settlers neglect to back the Americans, opting instead to mock them and insult their wine.

Oct. 13, 1812 The Americans are foiled yet again in their invasion attempt, as the War of 1812 leaves Canada in the hands of the British. Adding insult to injury, Canada burns down the White House and conquers Detroit. (Being good sports, they give it back.)

Jun. 15, 1846 The Oregon Boundary Treaty is signed, marking the 49th parallel as the boundary between Canada and the United States. Vancouver Island is left in the hands of the British, making future generations of crumpet-loving Canadian retirees very happy.

Nov. 17, 1860 The Grand Trunk Railway, an ambitious transcontinental railroad project, is completed—not to be confused with the American band Grand Funk Railroad, who would have a hit with "The Loco-Motion" 114 years later.

Mar. 29, 1867 Queen Victoria gives Canada a big cheerio with the signing of the British North America Act, forming the basis for modern-day Canada.

May 8, 1871 After two unsuccessful attempts at invasion, the U.S. simply asks Britain to *give* them Canada. Britain declines, but hey, the Americans still end up with the Treaty of Washington, granting them fishing rights in Canadian waters.

Feb. 23, 1893 A Canadian holy day. The first of many Lord Stanley's Cups is awarded to the Montreal AAA hockey team. Keep your Super Bowl and World Series; Stanley is the oldest trophy competed for by any professional sports team in North America.

Jul. 27, 1921 Clever Canucks Banting and Best isolate insulin and begin treating diabetes. Banting and fellow Canadian John Macleod shared the Nobel Prize for the discovery in 1923.

May 2, 1939 The National Film Board of Canada is created, paving the way for the evolution of documentaries, animation . . . and the smash hit *Porky's*.

Jun. 26, 1945 Canada joins the United Nations as a founding member.

Apr. 4, 1949 Canada joins NATO as a founding member.

Oct. 13, 1961 The introduction of the first universal coverage health plan in North America, leading to one of the most desirable health care systems in the world. And it all started in Saskatchewan!

1968 A landmark year for Canadian music with this trifecta—the release of Joni Mitchell's self-titled debut album, Robbie Robertson and The Band's instant classic *Music from Big Pink,* and perhaps most memorably, *The Transformed Man,* marking the singing debut of Montreal's William Shatner ("Take . . . that . . . Cohen.").

Sep. 28, 1972 Another Canadian hockey holy day. Paul Henderson becomes a household name as the man who scored the winning goal in the Canada vs. Soviet Hockey Series, known as the Summit on Ice.

Jul. 1, 1980 "O Canada" is declared Canada's national anthem, bringing to an end the uncertain hummings and mumblings that accompanied the start of most hockey games.

1982   A banner year in Canadian evolution. Canada brings home its very own constitution and brings into effect the Canadian Charter of Rights and Freedoms. We're pretty sure this all leads to the abolition of mushy peas and a relaxed view on pot and gay rights.

1988   A turbulent year in Canadian sports. Despite figure skater Kurt Browning's landing of the first quadruple toe loop in competition at the World Figure Skating Championship in Budapest, Canadian hearts break when a teary-eyed Wayne Gretzky gets traded to the Los Angeles Kings, and sprinter Ben Johnson is stripped of his record-setting 100m Gold Medal for steroid use. (Maybe if Kurt had landed two of them. . . .)

Jan. 1, 1989   The Free Trade Agreement between Canada and the U.S. goes into effect, paving the way for the North American Free Trade Agreement (NAFTA), in which Mexico is welcomed to the table. *Poutine* and Molsons for everybody!

Mar. 4, 1994   Canadian actor John Candy dies. A very sad day.

Dec. 3, 1997   Canada is the first country to sign the international treaty banning the use of landmines (signed in Ottawa).

Apr. 29, 1998 Canada signs the Kyoto Protocol, which commits industrialized nations to reduce emissions of greenhouse-effect gasses.

Apr. 1, 1999 In response to its Inuit population's desire for self-government, Canada officially declares the formation of the newest territory, Nunavut. (To get there from New York City, drive west until you hit North Dakota, then turn right and drive north for two days.)

Nov. 12, 2000 Canada decriminalizes marijuana for medicinal use.

Apr. 13, 2003 Canuck golfer Mike Weir keeps his cool to win the prestigious Masters Tournament in hot and muggy Augusta, Georgia.

Apr. 29, 2003 Prime Minister Jean Chrétien promises legislation to decriminalize possession of small amounts of marijuana. "Don't start to smoke yet," he says.

Jun. 13, 2003 Canada's highest court upholds the decision of the Ontario Court of Appeals, declaring the prohibition of same-sex marriage unconstitutional.

Aug. 1, 2004 *So, You Want to Be Canadian* is published to international acclaim. (Well, the authors' moms loved it.)

How to *Dress Like a Canadian*

Weary of low-rise jeans and tiny tees? Come to Canada, where bracing weather conditions prevent silly, skimpy fads and allow for the most accomplished of fashion trends: layering. Silk long johns paired with flannel: Fabulous! Turtlenecks topped with fisherman's sweaters: Cuddly! An all-red Union Suit with bottom flap? A classic! Mix and match different hues of Gortex, fleece, plaid, denim, wool, and cashmere for a plethora of different looks, all year 'round. Don't forget your toque—it looks good on everyone.

Did You Know?

Peelers (Canada's world-class and cold resistant strippers) can legally take it *all* off, even if the club serves liquor.

Toque:
Not just warm, but stylish

Down jacket:
Maintains body heat,
bulks up physique

Woolly scarf:
Conveniently adjustable
for beer consumption

Mittens:
Big on comfort,
small enough to
slip into cases of
your favorite brew

Snow pants:
The name says it all

Boots:
If you're not wearing these, you're wearing skates

Canadian Language
From Eh? to Zed

Why is Canadian language terrific?

 Cute accent makes dull statements sound adorable. Ask a Canadian to say, "out and about." (Everyone does.)

 Bilingual is better. English and French, as national languages, make for interesting cereal boxes, lotion bottles, and billboards. And go the extra mile to actually pronounce French words in French (it's foy-AY, not foyer).

 Canadians care about "u"—employing the romantic and literary British spellings—like harbour, colour, behaviour, etc.

 "Eh."

Did You Know?

Canadians say "zed" instead of "zee" when talking about the last letter of the alphabet.

The Story of Eh

Unlike its slow-witted cousin "huh," "eh" (pronounced AY) is a flexible, multipurpose word, perfect for a variety of situations. It also suits both of Canada's national languages, truly uniting two very different cultures with a single Canadian syllable. Its uses are endless, but as an example, adding *"eh?"* to the end of a statement is a handy and efficient substitute for:

This is just my opinion, but don't you agree with it?

Non-Canadian Statement: "The weather sure has turned chilly, don't you think?"
Canadian Statement: "Cold, eh?"

This is a fact to which anyone would acquiesce, so I'm being rhetorical here.

Non-Canadian Statement: "I can't believe you bought that girl a drink and she didn't even give you her number."
Canadian Statement: "That's cold, eh?"

You know what I just said? I actually believe the exact opposite.

Non-Canadian Statement: "Yes Bob, I agree it's very hot in Penticton today. I'm positively burning up."
Canadian Statement: "Right, cold, eh?"

A Brief Canadian Vocabulary Lesson

Ah jeez, I don't know about (a-BOOT) Pierre, he's been on pogey (POE-gee), won't get a joe job, and has no jing to go to the peelers. I mean, I've been feeding the hoser CCs at the pub so he won't put cheese in his coffee, but I think he's been spending a lot of time out-doors (OOT-doors) without (with-OOT) a toque (tewk). Either that, eh (ay), or his gonch is too tight.

American translation

Goodness gracious, I'm worried about Steve, he's been on unemployment, won't get an entry-level position, and doesn't have money to go to the strip clubs. You see, I've been buying that goof Canadian Club whisky so he won't go completely crazy, but I'm afraid he's lost the capacity to think. Perhaps the circulation to his brain has been cut off somehow.

How to *Apologize Like a Canadian*

So self-assured at all times and in all situations, and so empathetic to their fellow man, Canadians may apologize even when they are right. Try it yourself this week, and see how well-liked you become! Here's what to say . . .

. . . if you accidentally bump into someone:
Sorry! Sorry. My fault. Very sorry.

. . . if someone accidentally bumps into you:
Sorry! Sorry. My fault. Very sorry.

. . . if someone purposely and maliciously bumps into you:
Sorry! Sorry. My fault. Very sorry.

. . . if someone bumps into you, spills your coffee, trips you, and causes a minor concussion:
Sorry! Sorry. My fault. Very sorry.

Canadian

Culture

$\mathcal{C}anada$: Ready for Its Close-up

Who could forget the sweeping western landscape of
Wyoming in Clint Eastwood's Oscar-winning *Unforgiven*?
(Only that was actually Canada.) Who didn't want to move
to Montana, after seeing the scenic panoramas of *Legends
of the Fall*? (Only that was actually Canada.) Yes, it's true:
Canada is where Hollywood goes to shoot what America
wants to be.

MOVIE/TV SHOW	SET IN	FILMED IN
21 Jump Street	Hollywood	Vancouver
Aspen Extreme	Aspen, Colorado	British Columbia
Chicago	Chicago	Toronto
Elf	North Pole	Vancouver
The Hotel New Hampshire	New Hampshire	Quebec
Legends of the Fall	Montana	Alberta
Mission to Mars	Mars	Vancouver
Mystery, Alaska	Alaska	Alberta
Rumble in the Bronx	The Bronx	Ontario & B.C.
The Scarlet Letter	Massachusetts	Nova Scotia & B.C.
Smallville	Kansas	British Columbia
Unforgiven	Wyoming	Alberta
The X-Files	Spooky, alien-infested reality	British Columbia

Pizza Toppings—and Much More!

Canada's favorite films are named for its favorite meaty snacks.

Meatballs: Starring Bill Murray as a summer camp counselor, this Ivan Reitman comedy was the most successful Canadian movie ever when it was released in 1979.

Porky's: Usurping *Meatballs'* claim for most successful Canadian film ever in 1982, this classic teen sex comedy introduced young Canadian hottie Kim Cattrall (now famous for *Sex and the City*) as a horny high school teacher. Bonus: one of the lead male characters is named "Meat."

Canadian Bacon: Beloved Canadian comic and actor John Candy plays an American sheriff in this 1995 Michael Moore satire about a U.S. president who hopes to boost his sagging public approval ratings by starting a skirmish with Canada.

Did You Know?

After quietly serving as a scenic backdrop for umpteen American films, Canada finally won an Academy Award for the home team in 2004, winning Best Foreign Language Film for Denys Arcand's *The Barbarian Invasions*. His *Jesus of Montreal* was nominated in 1990, and his *Decline of the American Empire* in 1986.

Strange Brew

The strange odyssey of Bob and Doug McKenzie (played by Rick Moranis and Dave Thomas) began with the characters' first appearance on the great skit-comedy show *SCTV* in 1981. Created as a sarcastic way to fill two minutes of "Canadian" content required by the Canadian Broadcasting Corporation, the toque-wearing brothers swill beer, grill back bacon, muse about doughnuts, and speak in Canadianisms such as "beauty," "hoser," and "eh," all in front of a giant map of Canada. Inadvertently sparking a national craze, the actors quickly recorded an album of comedy bits (guest-starring Canadian rocker Geddy Lee of Rush). Their 1983 film debut, *Strange Brew,* in which the plucky Canadian underdogs outwit an evil brewmeister, is actually a clever reworking of *Hamlet*.

"Blame Canada"

This R-rated ditty from *South Park: Bigger, Longer and Uncut* received a surprise Oscar nomination for Best Original Song in 2000. In the lyrics, American parents search for a scapegoat for their children's bad language and behavior, exclaiming: "Should we blame the government?/ Should we blame society?/ Should we blame the images on TV?/ No! Blame Canada! Blame Canada!"

(World) Class Clowns

Canadians are funny. In fact, they are downright hilarious. If hockey is Canada's king, comedy reigns as its crown prince (no offense, England). For such a polite and inconspicuous group, Canadians have given the world comedic talents Dan Aykroyd, Mike Myers, Leslie Nielsen, the late Phil Hartman, and *Saturday Night Live* creator Lorne Michaels—and many more.

If you were too old for *SNL*, you probably loved *Wayne and Schuster;* too young, and you probably howled to the hi-jinks of the young Jim Carrey on *In Living Color*, or the inspired and outrageous comedy unit *The Kids in the Hall*. But beyond compare was *SCTV*. At its peak, the Toronto/ Edmonton incarnation of the *Second City* troupe transcended simple comedy and introduced comedic elements and characters that continue to inspire generations of comedians. With a cast that included Canadians John Candy, Martin Short, Eugene Levy, Catherine O'Hara, Andrea Martin, Dave Thomas, Rick Moranis, and Joe Flaherty, *SCTV* is a comic achievement that anyone in the world would be proud to call their own. But it's Canada's.

Oh, oh, oh Canada!

FAMOUS CANADIAN HOTTIES: GALS

Pamela Anderson: Born on Canada Day, as if on purpose, this *Baywatch* babe fittingly began her career as a Labatt's beer babe.

Kimberly Conrad Hefner: Forever famous for being the only woman Hef married—after he dated other Canadian Playboy Playmates Carrie Leigh and Shannon Tweed. They got hitched on Canada Day.

Dorothy Stratten: B.C.—born Playmate of the Year and lover of Peter Bogdanovich, Stratten's untimely death prompted several movies, including *Star 80*.

Shania Twain: Once upon a time, the award-winning, belly-baring country singer worked at a McDonald's in Timmins, Ontario.

Fay Wray: The blonde bombshell who tamed King Kong was born in mighty Alberta.

Margot Kidder: Easily the hottest of Lois Lanes, she hails from remote Yellowknife in the Northwest Territories.

Linda Evangelista: This feline supermodel is from Ontario.

Kim Cattrall: Hot gym teacher in *Porky's*; sexed-up Samantha in *Sex and the City*, raised on Vancouver Island.

Neve Campbell: The comeliest member of the *Party of Five*, this former ballerina was born in Guelph, Ontario.

Carrie-Anne Moss: This Vancouver babe guest-starred on *Due South* (see page 63) before kicking ass and taking names in *The Matrix*.

Elisha Cuthbert: *The Girl Next Door* babe and damsel-in-distress daughter to fellow Canuck Kiefer Sutherland on TV's *24*, hails from Calgary, Alberta.

FAMOUS CANADIAN HOTTIES: GUYS

Michael J. Fox: The compact cutie from *Family Ties* and *Back to the Future* hails from Edmonton, Alberta.

Corey Hart: If you don't know who he is, you weren't a teenager in the '80s. Or you didn't have a radio.

Jason Priestley: Mr. *90210* hails from British Columbia, not Beverly Hills.

Matthew Perry: The "funny one" on *Friends* is the son of a press aide to former Prime Minister babe Pierre Trudeau. American Dream moment—a brief fling with Julia Roberts.

Kiefer Sutherland: Before resurrecting his *Lost Boys* career with *24*, he too had a fling with Julia Roberts.

Did You Know?

Quizmasters Alex Trebek *(Jeopardy!)*, Jim Perry *(Card Sharks)*, and Monty Hall *(Let's Make a Deal)*–Canadians all!

Who Claims Keanu?

When discussing heartthrobs, Canada begrudgingly admits Keanu Reeves, who was raised in Toronto. When Keanu attempts to do a British accent on screen, however, Canadians are quick to point out he was actually born in Beirut and is not a Canadian citizen. (Note: Keanu's breakout movie *Speed* was written by true Canuck Graham Yost.)

Paul Gross: Born in Calgary, the *Due South*-er is even sexier than Dudley Do-Right (see page 63)—and scores extra points for not being a cartoon.

Peter Jennings: Since 1965, a reason for American women to stay awake for the news. (Not your type? Try White House correspondent John Roberts.)

Arthur Kent: "Scud Stud" during the first Gulf War, a new reason for American women to stay awake for the news.

Wayne Gretzky: He's the Great One. But he's also an Ontario-born Blond Babe who broke hearts across Canada when he married American blonde babe Janet Jones.

Alex Trebek: Some people think he's hot.

Wolverine: Okay, so he's fictional. But he's Canadian and, as embodied by Hugh Jackman, he's hot.

Who Can Teach the World to Sing?

Given its humble nature, it's easy to overlook Canada's contribution to the music scene. But Canadians are responsible for some of the world's best-selling pop and country hits, as well as the world's most influential singers-songwriters— including Leonard Cohen, Robbie Robertson, Neil Young, and Joni Mitchell—not to mention Anne Murray.

In fact, a Canadian was responsible for the world's most successful rock single: Kingston, Ontario, pop rocker Bryan Adams won this distinction in 1991 for his soft rock ballad "(Everything I Do) I Do It for You." Alanis Morissette, a native of Ottawa, Ontario, had the world's best-selling album by a female artist for 1995's *Jagged Little Pill.* In 2000, however, she was beat out by fellow Canuck, Shania Twain. Twain, already the world's best-selling country music artist in history, now holds the distinction of best-selling album by a female solo artist for *Come on Over.*

Why is Canadian music—like its citizens—so universally appealing? Perhaps because, just as it welcomes all types of people, Canada embraces all sorts of musicians, from Halifax indie grunge to Montreal lounge acts to Vancouver folk rock. Like over-the-top pop ballads? Celine Dion is at the ready. Need a fix of angry, angst-ridden love songs? Try Avril Lavigne. (Over 21? Try Peaches.) Feeling the urge for a bittersweet melody on a rainy Sunday afternoon? Sarah McLachlan is your girl. Miss your 1970s glory days? BTO is still rockin' "You Ain't Seen Nothin' Yet" on a Canadian stage somewhere. And you haven't truly experienced Canadian music until you've bounced up and down in unison to Great Big Sea at a kitchen party, feeling the love in a whole different way than at a rave. It's a beautiful thing.

Did You Know?

Despite "American Woman"'s lyrical bite ("American woman, stay away from meee-heee"), it was Canadian rockers The Guess Who's only stateside No.1 hit, spending three weeks at the top. When the group was invited to play the White House for President Nixon, First Lady Pat asked the group not to play the song, and they complied with typical Canadian politesse.

The All-Time, All-Canadia

Alanis Morissette, "You Oughta Know"

Avril Lavigne, "Complicated"

Anne Murray, "Snowbird"

Bachman-Turner Overdrive, "Takin' Care of Business"

The Band, "Up on Cripple Creek"

Barenaked Ladies, "One Week"

Blue Rodeo, "Try"

Broken Social Scene, "Stars and Sons"

Bryan Adams, "(Everything I Do) I Do It for You"

Celine Dion, "My Heart Will Go On"

Corey Hart, "Sunglasses at Night"

Cowboy Junkies, "Misguided Angel"

The Crash Test Dummies, "Mmm Mmm Mmm Mmm"

D.O.A., "Disco Sucks"

Diana Krall, "When I Look in Your Eyes"

Gordon Lightfoot, "Sundown"

Great Big Sea, "Consequence Free"

The Guess Who, "American Woman"

Smash Hit Parade

Joni Mitchell, "Big Yellow Taxi"

k. d. lang, "Constant Craving"

Leonard Cohen, "Suzanne"

Loverboy, "Working for the Weekend"

Men Without Hats, "Safety Dance"

Neil Young, "Heart of Gold"

Paul Anka, "Lonely Boy"

Peaches, "Set It Off"

Robbie Robertson, "Sacrifice"

Rush, "Tom Sawyer"

Sarah Harmer, "Basement Apartment"

Sarah McLachlan, "Building a Mystery"

Shania Twain, "(If You're Not in It for Love) I'm Outta Here!"

Skinny Puppy, "Smothered Hope"

The Tragically Hip, "New Orleans Is Sinking"

The Unicorns, "I Was Born a Unicorn"

William Shatner, "Lucy in the Sky with Diamonds"

Snowbird
vs.
The Snowbirds

Golden-throated Canadian singer Anne (Snowbird) Murray rocked the world in 1970 when her hit single "Snowbird" achieved major fame, winning an unprecedented number of international awards. Canada is also the birthplace of The Snowbirds, an elite air demonstration unit based on the 431st Bomber Squadron—also the recipient of many international honors. In conversation, please take care to not confuse the two. As you'll see from this table, they're actually quite different. Let's compare.

	Snowbird	The Snowbirds
Longevity	Born June 20, 1945, in Springhill, Nova Scotia	Born November 11, 1942, in Dartmouth, Nova Scotia
Endurance	Fourteen performances across North America in December '03 alone	On average, six shows a month
Velocity	Her sweet, sweet melodies hit the ear at the speed of sound	One-on-one flybys achieve a closure speed just *below* the speed of sound
Mass	Approximately 137 pounds, soaking wet	7170 pounds, fully gassed

The Legend of Stompin' Tom

Stompin' Tom Connors is a folk hero—an everyman singer-songwriter who is fiercely Canadian. He never, ever tried to be a rock star, and therefore earned his country's undying admiration. Armed with a guitar, a cowboy hat, a twang, and a piece of plywood for stomping on, Tom wasn't afraid of hokey ditties about whatever town he was in at the time. Lore has it that Tom—the pride of Prince Edward Island— sang his first song for a glass of beer he couldn't afford, and that his trademark traveling plywood plank (from Canadian hardware chain Beaver Lumber) was first employed because he was pounding right through the stage floor while keeping a beat. To date, he has more than two-dozen albums and a devoted national following who belt out lyrics to his timeless tunes: "The Ketchup Song," "Bud the Spud," "The Hockey Song," and "Canada Day, Up Canada Way."

Did You Know?

Canadian Sarah McLachlan was the driving force behind Lilith Fair, the all-female-performer music festival.

Invented in Canada

MAKING THE WORLD A BETTER PLACE

Imagine a world with nothing but buttons. Then, thank goodness for crafty Canadians, who invented the zipper, not to mention a long list of other essentials that would be impossible to live without. Here is but a small sampling of Canuck ingenuity at work.

- The Abdominizer

- Air hockey: Naturally.

- Antigravity suit

- Basketball: Invented by James Naismith, of Ontario

- Canadarm: Cleverly named to ensure the proper country received credit, this fifteen-meter Remote Manipulator System is an essential tool on the space shuttle and brings the maple leaf logo to alien life forms everywhere.

- Chocolate bar: A fishing trip prompted chocolatiers Arthur Ganong and George Ensor to invent a chocolate nut bar, which they began selling in New Brunswick in 1910.

Dental mirror

Documentary film: Canada's *Nanook of the North* (1922) was the first film ever termed a "documentary." And perhaps, the first film that ever offered you a much-need nap in grade school.

Five-pin bowling

Frozen fish fillets: Believe it or not, it took until 1929 before someone—namely Dr. Archibald G. Huntsman— had the brilliant idea to sell "Ice Fillets" to the public. Alberta housewives celebrate by bringing trout in off the back porch.

Fuller Brush Company: Mr. Fuller, the father of door-to-door sales, was born in Nova Scotia.

Ginger Ale: Invented in 1904 by University of Toronto chemist and pharmacist John J. McLaughlin, his "Pale Dry Ginger Ale," featuring a beaver sitting atop a map of Canada on every can, was the predecessor to Canada Dry, still the "champagne of ginger ales" and the perfect partner to Canadian whisky (see page 72).

Plastic garbage bags

Goalie mask: Naturally.

Hydrofoil boat

Ice hockey: The first recorded game took place on Christmas Day, 1855, in Kingston, Ontario, when bored members of the Royal Canadian Rifles tied blades to their boots, borrowed field hockey sticks and a lacrosse ball, and hit the frozen harbor. Appropriately, the International Hockey Hall of Fame is located in Kingston.

IMAX movie system

Instant mashed potatoes: As of 1962, spud-loving campers everwhere notice a significant lightening of their backpacks.

Insulin: Isolated by Canadians to treat diabetes.

Java programming language

Jet Ski

Jolly Jumper: An essential parenting tool, this "helpful harness" hooks on a door frame and lets active babies bounce for hours without spilling their parents' Caesars.

Lacrosse: Originally played by the Algonquian Indian tribes in Canada's St. Lawrence Valley (who considered it a religious rite and warrior training), lacrosse is North America's oldest organized sport. The Lacrosse Hall of Fame is in B.C.

💡 *Lawn sprinkler*

💡 *Lightbulb*: Contrary to many history lessons, the first electric lightbulb lamp was patented by Toronto med student Henry Woodward, who in 1875 sold a share in the patent to an American (and son of a Canadian ex-pat) named Thomas Edison, who obviously ran with it.

💡 *Paint roller*

💡 *Prosthetic hand*

💡 *Snowmobile*

💡 *Snowplough*: Note the proper spelling

💡 *Snowblower*

💡 *Short-wave radio*

💡 *Square-head ("Robertson") screwdriver*

Did You Know?

Yahtzee was invented by a wealthy Canadian couple to pass the time with friends on their yacht (thus its original name, "The Yacht Game").

Standard time: Though critics dubbed it "against the will of God" in 1879, Canadian Sir Sanford Fleming introduced the concept of international standard time zones. Today, British relatives still call way too early on Sunday mornings.

Superman: The world's most famous superhero—and ironically, the enduring symbol of American strength—was co-created by Canadian Joe Shuster and American Jerome Siegel.

Did You Know?

The Daily Planet, the newspaper Clark Kent and Lois Lane worked for, was originally dubbed *The Daily Star*—an homage to Superman co-creator Joe Shuster's job at the *Toronto Star*. It was only changed after DC Comics bought syndication rights. Note the actress who played Lois Lane in the original 1978 movie was also a Canadian (see page 41).

Telephone: Debate about which country can claim the phone still rages, as Alexander Graham Bell moved from Canada to the states while actively working on it. Diplomatically, he said at the time, "The telephone was conceived in Brantford (Ontario) in 1874 and born in Boston in 1875." Canada: happy to be the land of conception.

Trivial Pursuit (as well as Scruples, Balderdash, Pictionary, and Yahtzee): Q: Does cold weather breed multimillion-selling board games? A: Looks like it, eh?

YMCA: The first one in North America opened in Montreal in 1951, the second in Boston a month later.

Zamboni: You know, those things that smooth the ice in skating and hockey rinks.

Zipper

CANADIAN
Beasties

A delightful array of critters and exotic beasties live in Canada. Can you blame them for making Canada their home?

Ogopogo: Canada's answer to the Loch Ness monster, the Ogopogo—called *N'ha-a-itk* in native Salish—lives in B.C.'s Lake Okanagan. Regular sightings of the Ogopogo continue to this day, though like her Scottish cousin, she usually shies from the camera.

Bonhomme: Fully dubbed Bonhomme Carnaval, this living incarnation of a snowman has enchanted Quebec youngsters for generations. Unlike the Ogopogo, he loves to pose for photos and can be found—in his traditional red toque and belt—at Quebec's winter carnival.

Beaver: It may be the world's second largest rodent, but it's number one in Canada's heart. Chosen for its industriousness and fortitude (and probably also for those cute front teeth), it's the country's official national animal.

Moose: Southern-bred sissy drivers who swerve to miss a deer on the road have probably never had to face down the mighty moose. A typical specimen weighs in at over 2,500 pounds (that's 1,134 kilograms in Canada)—the weight of about fifty beavers! Much to the chagrin of the noble beaver, the moose is often thought of as the country's mascot.

Did You Know?
The plural for moose is moose.

Canadian goose: With synchronized flight patterns mimicked by elite jet pilots and Tour de France cyclists, Canadian geese also evoke admiration for their fearless annual pilgrimage to crap on the U.S.

Sasquatch: Although some U.S. residents, mostly hippies living near Seattle, believe this to be an American creature, Sasquatch clearly relishes roaming above the 49th parallel. In his honor, Kokanee beer hides his likeness on every delicious can.

Glooscap: Huge in size and power, this mythic woodsman of the Eastern Woodland Indians is believed by some to be the predecessor of legendary lumberjack Paul Bunyan.

Johnny Canuck: Kind of the Uncle Sam of Canada, this fearless strongman appeared in nineteenth-century cartoons; more recently, he evolved into Captain Canuck, a superhero sporting a patriotic maple leaf on his forehead.

Ookpik: The name means Happy Little Arctic Owl. This brave stuffed toy, made of ultra-cuddly sealskin, selflessly waddled away from Canadian popularity into Canadian lore. Disappearance of the toys in the '70s is believed to have single-handedly increased the national seal population.

Loup-Garou: A werewolf in French-Canadian folktales; the transformation from human to wolf is punishment for seven years of skipping mass. (That'll teach you to sleep in on Sundays.)

Windigo: The spirit believed by the Algonquian to take possession of vulnerable persons, causing them to engage in various types of antisocial behavior, most notably cannibalism, after being in the woods.

Did You Know?

In 1965, Canadian fiddler extraordinaire Frankie Rodgers composed the lovely, now standard "Ookpik Waltz" in honor of the plucky little owl.

All About

Polite, charming, and sporting good posture, the northern heroes known as the Royal Canadian Mounted Police (hence, "Mounties") fight crime, return lost kittens, and reassure Canadians that their world is safe—all while wearing those devastatingly handsome red uniforms.

Mounties

Hat designed for frequent tipping

Shiny buttons!

Noble Canadian chin

Excellent posture
exudes confidence

Polite and
friendly steed

Everyone loves a man in a uniform!

The Story
of
Mounties

Mounties were born in 1873 as the North West Mounted Police—they didn't become the RCMP until 1920—and were charged with not just the protection of the Yukon and its gold, but with establishing good relationships with the indigenous population of Canada's great western frontier. Not surprisingly, the Wild West that is so often portrayed in movies was far more calm, cool, and collected in Canada, as the Mounties paved the way for the settlement of the west by negotiation and trust before resorting to shoot-'em-ups. The Mounties' politesse became a calling card of Canadians, and one that remains prominent in the national character. And if you're looking for films celebrating the mythology of this crimson-clad troop of crime-fighters, you'll most likely have to look south. Due to their unwaver- ing modesty, Canadians prefer to let others whisper admiringly about their exploits. It's all in a day's work.

DUDLEY DO-RIGHT OF THE MOUNTIES

In 1961, the flaxen-haired, giant-chinned pride of the RCMP debuted in living rooms. (He's the creation of *Rocky and Bullwinkle* mastermind Jay Ward.) Although studly Dudley regularly rode his horse backwards and found himself fired, he—in true Canadian style—always returned to politely and nonviolently save the day from evil-doer Snidely Whiplash.

Due South

TV's *Due South* (1994–98) starred Calgary-born hunk Paul Gross as an RCMP liaison in Chicago. Appropriately, the hat-tipping and crisply enunciating Mountie got his man via excellent tracking skills, good manners, and the ability to withstand freezing temperatures—as opposed to the brasher methods of his gun-wielding American counterpart. He often quotes Inuit lore from Canada's Northwest Territories, and his catch phrase is "thank you kindly." Like Dudley Do-Right, the show retains a cult following of women who love a Canadian in uniform.

& Beer!

(and Poutine)

Eating
and Drinking
in Canada

If you want to eat like a Canadian, sample a variety of cuisines from all over the world—because just as Canadians welcome people of diverse cultures to their country, they also welcome their food. The key to making your dining experience truly "Canadian" is to wash it down with a cold, frosty Canadian beer. Drinking, after all, is widely recognized as the "eating" of Canada. Feel free to skip ahead to that section (see page 71).

If you do decide to eat something, you'll note that much like the disposition of its residents, Canadian staples are unbelievably sweet. Some favorites:

Butter tart: A mini pecan pie with raisins instead of pecans. Popular as a coffee-time snack at Tim Hortons, especially when you're tired of glazed doughnuts.

Nanaimo bar: Named for a town on Vancouver Island, it's a layered dessert with graham cracker crust, dense sugar-cream middle, and chocolate topping.

Maple fudge: Fudge, but maple flavored. You get it.

Tire sur la neige: Maple syrup tapped straight from the tree, boiled, and poured on snow to form a taffy-like confection, often eaten at a *cabane-à-sucre* (a seasonal treat shop).

Beaver tail: Canada's answer to the elephant ear, a popular deep-fried, sugar-dusted carnival treat (see page 70).

Three notable, salty exceptions to the sweet rule are *poutine*, *eggs benny* (exactly like Eggs Benedict, but Canadian), and *back bacon* (you didn't think they called it "Canadian bacon" in Canada, did you?). Canadians also love dousing things in vinegar.

POUTINE (POO-TEEN): MEAL OF THE BRAVE

Sure, it may look like a big platter of goo, but *poutine* is an international taste sensation that floors fragile visitors and satisfies hearty Canadians even more than also-popular Canadian KD (Kraft Dinner), especially at 3 A.M. Mmmm!

STEP 1: Get some fries.

STEP 2: Pour hot gravy over fries.

STEP 3: Top with cheese curds.

STEP 4: Broil and serve with your favorite accoutrement, such as ketchup or hot sauce.

Did You Know?

Poutine is the perfect food to scarf while enjoying the munchies-inducing masterworks of Cheech Marin and Tommy Chong (born in Edmonton, Alberta), including *Up in Smoke* (1978), *Cheech & Chong's Next Movie* (1980), *Cheech & Chong's Nice Dreams* (1981), and many more.

Moose Stroganoff

1½ pounds moose steak, diced

½ cup plus 2 tablespoons flour

1 teaspoon salt

1 clove garlic

2 small onions, chopped

½ pounds mushrooms, chopped

1 tablespoon Worcestershire sauce

1 cup beef bouillon

1 cup sour cream

1 pound egg noodles

Just like Mom used to make.
(serves a family of 4)

Coat the meat in ¼ cup flour and salt. In a frying pan, sauté garlic, onions, and mushrooms in fat for 5 minutes. Add meat and cook until brown. Remove meat, mushrooms, and onions from the pan. Set aside. Add the remaining flour to the juices in the pan. Stir in Worcestershire and bouillon. Cook to reduce until the sauce thickens. Add the sour cream. Heat until gravy simmers. Return the moose and vegetables to the pan. Stir to combine and reheat. Serve over cooked and drained egg noodles.

Did You Know?

James Lewis Kraft, cheese genius and founding father behind the Canadian staple Kraft Dinner, was born in Stevensville, Ontario.

Beaver Tail

1 beaver tail
(about 1 pound)

A frontier favorite.
(serves 4 as an appetizer)

Roast the beaver tail over campfire until tender and the skin begins to loosen, about 15 minutes. Remove skin. Cut into bite-sized portions. Enjoy.

Beaver Tail with Beans (B & B)

1 beaver tail
(about 1 pound)

Two 14-ounce
cans of
baked beans

1 medium onion,
chopped

Salt and pepper

B&B is best enjoyed downwind.
(serves 3 hungry lumberjacks)

Cook the beaver tail over fire, until skin loosens. Remove skin. Cut meat into bite-size pieces. In a pot, place beans, beaver meat, and onion. Bring to a boil, reduce heat to medium, and simmer for 45 minutes, stirring occasionally. Add salt and pepper to taste.

Beaver Tail Pastry

This delicious Canadian treat is best appreciated alfresco. Here's how you can experience the magic.

1. Find a Canadian carnival.
2. Follow the trail of powdered sugar.
3. Say to the food vendor, "One piping-hot tail, please."
4. Hand over a toonie.
5. Enjoy.

Drink!

It's funny; although Canadian beer is only marginally stronger than American beer, everyone thinks the alcohol level is much higher because it tastes so much better. Maybe it's because Canadians retain ties to their beer-loving mother country, Britain. Maybe it's because Canada is a nation of beer experts—beer accounts for a whopping 83 percent of all alcohol sold in Canada. And the average Canadian bought 85.3 liters of beer last year. (Come on over—we've got Kokanee in the fridge!)

While Molson reigns supreme as North America's oldest beer maker (founded in Montreal by John Molson in 1786), Canadians also relish Kokanee, Labatt's Blue, Labatt's Blue Light, Moosehead, Alexander Keith's, and Schooner. The latter is named for the 1920s champion sailing schooner *Bluenose*, which trounced the U.S. for seventeen years in a row to win the International Fisherman's Cup, and which still reigns supreme on the front of the Canadian dime.

Q: **WHAT DO CANADIANS DRINK WHEN THEY'RE NOT DRINKING BEER?**

A: **THEY DRINK WHISKY.**

Canadian whisky, often called "rye" for short, is a blend of straight whiskys (usually rye corn and barley) distilled only in Canada under government supervision. Popular brands include Crown Royal and Canadian Club. If it's too strong for you as-is, a Canadian was nice enough to invent ginger ale to go with it (see page 51). Ask for a "Rye and Ginger."

Did You Know?

The handles on Canadian beer cases are big enough to fit your hands with mittens on.

Handy Liquor Vocabulary

TWO-FOUR: 24 beers, as opposed to a case of 12. Also called a "two-fer" or a "flat." (A six-pack? Come on! Most Canadians will show up to a party—or an afternoon in front of the game, or a christening—with "four times the fun.")

STUBBIES: The distinctive, short-necked beer bottles that were once the Canadian standard. Sadly, they are now rare, but many lobby for their return.

MICKEY: A pint liquor bottle, perfect for stashing in the pocket of a flannel shirt.

40 POUNDER: The bigger liquor bottle, like America's "fifth" size.

How to Drink Like a Canadian

Canadians are so thoughtful that they've crafted a refreshing alcoholic beverage for any time of the day. If you want to drink like a Canadian, check your watch and order one of the favorites listed here.

9 A.M. Order a Calgary Red Eye. Canadian beer and tomato juice, sometimes with an egg added; also called "Breakfast of Champions."

NOON Order a Bloody Caesar. Perfect to take the chill off cold Canadian mornings is this elixir, often called Canada's national cocktail. It was invented in Calgary in 1969 by Walter Chell, who mashed fresh clams into tomato juice to make the drink. Now, you can use Clamato, which is much quicker. Three Caesars equals brunch in many provinces.

2 P.M. Order a Blue. That's Labatt's to me and you.

4 P.M. Order Yellow Snow. In some provinces, a term for beer. Just be careful what you're asking for, especially in the winter months.

5 P.M. Order a Screech. The official drink of Newfoundland, this cheap, lethally strong rum was developed from a centuries-old rum-for-salt-fish trade with Jamaica. Try it and you'll quickly understand the name.

6 P.M. *Order an Ice Wine.* Very chilly wine grapes from the Okanagan Valley make for very sweet, very strong Canadian wine.

6:15 P.M. *Order a CC.* Shorthand for Canadian Club whisky. Useful at the bar when you just can't get out another syllable.

6:30 P.M. *Repeat till bedtime.*

Hail Caesar!

The Perfect Bloody Caesar

celery salt	
6 ounces Clamato juice	Coat the rim of a tall glass with celery salt. Add the rest of the ingredients and stir. Serve on the rocks. Garnish with a celery stalk and lime wedge.
1 1/2 ounces vodka	
1 dash Worcestershire sauce	
1 dash Tabasco sauce	
1 pinch horseradish	
pepper to taste	
celery stalk	
lime wedge	

key

and

More Hockey

followed by

TALK OF HOCKEY

(Canadian Sports)

Canada: Land of Good Sports

Other countries may foolishly believe that ice hockey is an international sport, but Canada—the country where modern hockey was born—knows the truth. Since lucky Canada is a winter wonderland nearly nine months of the year, it's great at raising athletes who balance on ice from toddlerhood and are seemingly impervious to cold. In Canadian households, there's no debating whether the kids should play soccer, baseball, football, or basketball. They get sticks for Christmas, and they play hockey. A thrilling hockey tableau even graces the back of the Canadian five dollar bill.

Hockey 101

Hockey is the common language of Canada, and it's nice not to have to bother with mixed metaphors from a variety of sports. Everyone—*everyone*—knows what you're talking about when you say these things while watching the game:

- **"Ah jeez, I miss the days of Gretzky in his office."** (Not a business analogy, but a reference to how the Great One pioneered play behind the net, a location known as His Office.)

- **"He's gone down to block one too many shots without his helmet."** (He's crazy.)

- **"He undressed that guy!"** Or, alternatively, **"He left him standing in his gonch!"** (He's been out maneuvered.)

"You can't put the puck in the net without spending some time in the corners." (Sage advice about working for your payoffs.)

"He stood on his head on that one/he's playing unconscious." (Similar to Canadian Keanu Reeves in *The Matrix*, using uncanny dexterity to keep opponents at bay.)

"They're no '84 Oilers." (Useful for any occasion when a team is down, because everyone agrees that *no one* is like the '84 Oilers. For variety, and depending on age, you can replace with '77 or '56 Canadiens.)

"He's droppin' the gloves, eh?" (Signifies the beginning of a fight, otherwise known as, "honest negotiations on a difference of opinion.")

"Ah, it's not a bad game, but it's not old-time hockey." (Your go-to phrase, perfect in any hockey situation, even if you have no idea what's going on.)

Did You Know?

The Edmonton Dynasty is not a nighttime Canadian soap opera, but a reference to the great hockey lineage of Edmonton, Alberta.

HOW TO USE HOCKEY TERMINOLOGY
in Romantic Situations

Of course, this common palette of hockey metaphors naturally extends from the ice to the boudoir (that's French-Canadian for The Bedroom), effectively bridging Canada's two favorite winter pastimes. Use this handy vocabulary when describing your next dating adventure:

HOCKEY TERM *Lighting the lamp*
DEFINITION A red light has been turned on by the goal judge to indicate the puck has successfully crossed the line
USE IN ROMANTIC CONTEXT To "score"; have sex (also known as "putting the puck in the net")

HOCKEY TERM *Fanning the puck*
DEFINITION Missing contact when attempting a shot
USE IN ROMANTIC CONTEXT Blowing the opportunity to "light the lamp" (see above); often shortened to, "Ah jeez, he fanned it"

HOCKEY TERM *Pulling the goalie*
DEFINITION Removing your goaltender in return for an extra attacker on the ice, often in desperation to "light the lamp"
USE IN ROMANTIC CONTEXT Spanking the monkey, choking the chicken, or the more PETA-friendly term, masturbation (also known as "playing with an extra attacker")

HOCKEY TERM *Going 5-hole*
DEFINITION Shooting toward the space between the goalie's two leg pads, often the target for an astute player
USE IN ROMANTIC CONTEXT See "lighting the lamp," specifically, getting between the legs

HOCKEY TERM *Bobby Orr*
DEFINITION The legendary defenseman who happened to play with one stripe of tape on his stick
USE IN ROMANTIC CONTEXT A particular bikini-wax style often seen in Canadian peeler bars

HOCKEY TERM *The wingman (or winger)*
DEFINITION The player whose hard work allows someone else to score on the ice
USE IN ROMANTIC CONTEXT The player whose hard work allows someone else to score in the bar

Hockey Hair: The Misunderstood Mullet

Unlike other world citizens, who might sport a mullet as simply a trendy hairstyle, this Canadian crown is worn with both a nationalistic *and* a practical purpose—it honors the sloping silhouette of the beaver, and it keeps the back of the neck warm and doesn't interfere with one's vision through one's hockey helmet.

figure 1.

figure 2.

WHAT TO DO
WHEN YOU'RE NOT PLAYING HOCKEY

Play Lacrosse: Like hockey without the ice, or the pads.

Play Football: Canadian Football League players battle in snow and mud for the coveted Grey Cup. They play for glory—rarely for huge contracts.

Play Rugby: Hockey and lacrosse not tough enough for you?

Go Skiing: Downhill, free-style, cross-country.

Go Curling: Think it's not a sport? You try running down a sheet of ice.

Go Ice Fishing: Catch 'em. Cook 'em. Eat 'em.

Perform Synchronized Swimming Maneuvers: The sport originated from a series of movements executed by the Canadian Royal Lifesaving Society, with the first competition held in Montreal in 1923.

Did You Know?

The winner of the 2003 Rock-Paper-Scissors International World Championship, Canadian Rob Krueger, took the title by employing the brilliant Fistful of Dollars Gambit (rock-paper-paper).

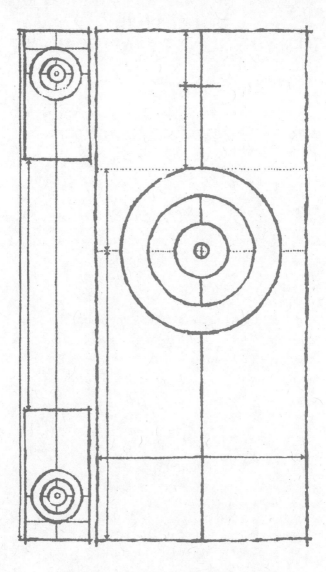

Curling: You can do it drunk!

Curling IT'S NOT HOCKEY, BUT IT'S FUN

Sometimes wrongly confused with frozen bowling, this wild winter sport requires a renaissance sportsman. It's a little like hockey, a little like chess, a little like shuffleboard, and a lot like mopping the floor. In 1911, Winnipeg became the center for Canadian curling, and the hotly contested Air Canada Silver Broom was established as the world curling championship in 1968. (Canada proceeded to win the first five competitions.) Today, curling is still an exhilarating, passionate Olympic sport that showcases the innate ability of Canadians to think in cold weather, properly match their sweater sets, and balance on ice. A whopping 98 percent of Canadians can curl while legally drunk.

Did You Know?

Montreal Canadien superstar Maurice "Rocket" Richard is the only NHL player to have spawned a riot (when he was suspended from the 1955 Stanley Cup Playoffs), a permanent interactive tourist attraction (Univers Maurice Richard in Montreal), and a Grecian Formula ad (with the now-immortal line, "Hey Richard, that's two minutes for looking so good!")

How to Celebrate

It could be said that if you are lucky enough to live in the greatest country in the world, every day is "Canada Day," but there is also a special holiday that bears this distinction. Here's how to live it up and pay your respects, Canuck style, all year-round.

HERITAGE DAY –3RD Monday of February

What It Is: Established in 1973 by the Heritage Canada Foundation, this holiday encourages the "preservation and promotion of Canada's nationally significant historic, architectural, natural, and scenic heritage."

How to Celebrate: Flip on the game (don't you dare ask which sport) and fill up on *poutine,* ice wine, and beaver tails. During intermission, discuss insulin, the Battle of 1812, the Oilers, and the Rocky Mountains.

Did You Know?

Canadians drink an estimated 150 million bottles of beer on Victoria Day weekend each year.

Like a Canadian

VICTORIA DAY – May 24 (varies if the 24th is a Sunday)

What It Is: Originally the birthday of Queen Victoria (1837–1901), the holiday was made official in Canada in 1845, and is now used as a generic day for celebrating the birthdays of subsequent monarchs.

How to Celebrate: Hitch up your bloomers, tipple some tea, and belt out a rousing rendition of "We are the Champions," my friend.

NATIONAL ABORIGINAL DAY – June 21

What It Is: Declared official in 1996 and held on the summer solstice, National Aboriginal Day celebrates the First Nations, Inuit, and Métis people with festivals and traditional music and dance. Special events take place at Head-Smashed-In Buffalo Jump, a UNESCO World Heritage Site in Alberta where native North Americans hunted bison by chasing them off a cliff.

How to Celebrate: Nothing says "party" like buffalo wings, berries, ice cream, and some good old-fashioned dancing around the fire.

CANADA DAY – July 1

What It Is: Established as "Dominion Day" in 1879, this national holiday celebrates the anniversary of Canada's formation as a union in 1867.

How to Celebrate: This is the big one. Head outside for some back bacon grilling, fireworks, and a frosty mug (or six) of Canada's finest, beer.

THANKSGIVING – 2nd Monday of October

What It Is: Initially created to praise the end of wars and cholera, this holiday has evolved into its present-day *raison d'etre*—humble thanks for all things Canadian.

How to Celebrate: Sleep in late, throw a turkey in the oven, stir up some Caesars, and head out for some shinny (pick-up hockey) to work up an appetite for the evening feast.

MUMMERING –a.k.a. The Twelve Days of Christmas

What It Is: In this old British custom still practiced in rural Newfoundland, "mummers" dress up in old clothes to disguise their identity and visit their neighbors for singing and dancing. The hosts usually supply Christmas cake and syrup and a glass of "grog"—a drink made with rum or whisky—while trying to guess the identities of their masked visitors.

How to Celebrate: If it ain't broke, don't fix it: Pour the screech and dance, rummy!

BOXING DAY – December 26

What It Is: Also known as the Feast of St. Stephen, Boxing Day may have come from the tradition of opening of church "poor boxes" the day after Christmas and distributing their contents to those less fortunate. Today, it's more about the shopping—but still a time to give small gifts to those who've provided service, and to donate to those in need.

How to Celebrate: Get the envelope ready for the paper-boy/girl, drop off that bag of hockey gear at your local charity, and hit the after-Christmas sales with reckless abandon.

Did You Know?

Held over three weekends in February for more than a quarter century, Ottawa's Winterlude Festival celebrates the joys of the Canadian winter and is hosted by a family of furry, magical "ice hogs."

O Canada

Proclaimed Canada's national anthem on July 1, 1980, "O Canada" was first sung 100 years before, on June 24, 1880. The music was composed by Calixa Lavallée, then known as "Canada's national musician," to accompany a poem written in French by judge Adolphe-Basile Routhier. The English lyrics are based on a 1908 poem by Montreal lawyer and author Robert Stanley Weir. Sing it with pride at hockey games or just to liven things up at parties (please stand and remove your toque).

English

O Canada!
Our home and native land,
True patriot love in all thy sons command.

With glowing hearts we see thee rise,
The True North strong and free!

From far and wide,
O Canada, we stand on guard for thee.

God keep our land glorious and free!
O Canada, we stand on guard for thee.
O Canada, we stand on guard for thee.

Français

O Canada!
Terre de nos aïeux,
Ton front est ceint de fleurons glorieux!

Car ton bras sait porter l'épée,
Il sait porter la croix!

Ton histoire est une épopée
Des plus brillants exploits.

Et ta valeur, de foi trempée,
Protégera nos foyers et nos droits.
Protégera nos foyers et nos droits.

Clip and fly the Canadian flag with pride.
Let the world know . . .

I

♥

Canada!

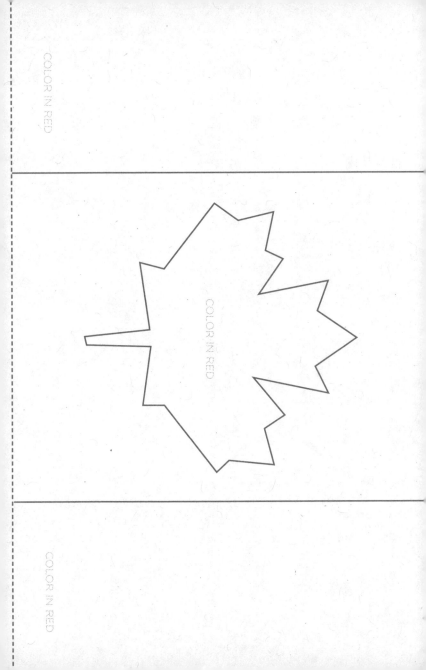

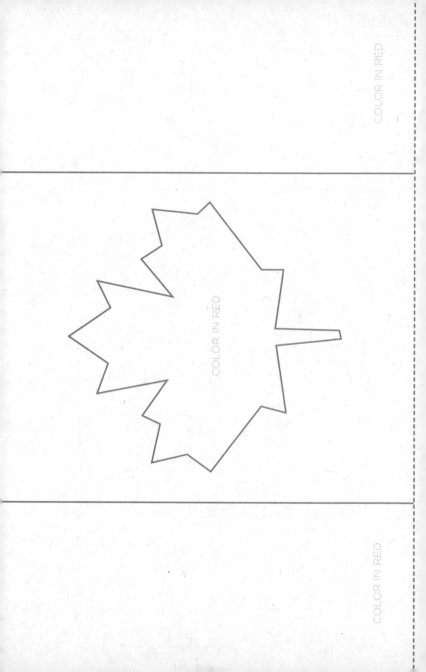

COLOR IN RED

COLOR IN RED

COLOR IN RED

COLOR IN RED

For encouragement and inspiration, the authors would like to thank their families and friends (including Baz, Cody, Eck, Fall, Metal, Nev, Shew, Shuck, Spute, Trio, Vegas, and the rest of you who truly represent the soul of Canada); Steve Mockus, Sara Gillingham, and the whole gang at Chronicle Books and Raincoast Books (we owe each of you a Kokanee); the Edmonton cast of *SCTV*; Stompin' Tom Connors; and, last but definitely not least, the '84 Oilers.

Kerry Colburn is the author of *The Rebound Journal, My Fabulous Life,* and *My Dysfunctional Life* (all from Chronicle Books). She lives in San Francisco, and wants to be Canadian so much that she married her co-author.

Rob Sorensen originally hails from Edmonton, Alberta (famous for the Great One, Wayne Gretzky). Although he currently hangs his toque in San Francisco, he still faithfully drinks Crown Royal, roots for the Oilers, and celebrates Canada Day.

visit **www.soyouwanttobecanadian.com,** eh?